The Shepherd of Olympus

CORY B. SCOTT

ISBN: 9781797774732

DEDICATION

This small book is dedicated to my bigger than life family. Karen my wife, Alexandrea and Samantha my daughters, and my Grandson Bean. May we all finish this life well and with as few Micas or Cellardoor's as possible.

CONTENTS

ACKNOWLEDGMENTS

I want to acknowledge the Old Shepherd who has made this life so much more tolerable since he and I have come back into each other's hearts.

DISCLAIMER

This story is obviously a work of fiction, I mean, who has ever seen a war wolf? Besides, we know that the many Olympus type organizations out there would never take advantage of a naive true believer; much less, sacrifice one to protect their own reputation. So, with that in mind, if you see, or read, anything that resembles actual real-life situations, come on, you know better. Just caulk it up as a coincidence, and let's all just move on.

INTRODUCTION

Britney was running so fast to the sound of an attack on her sheep that she ran headlong into something she had never seen in the grasslands before. The monster was busy devouring its prey as she ran headlong into it, so hard she bounced off the creature and landed on her back, in the grass. The massive animal seemed unaffected by the sudden impact. It barely took notice of the disturbance, but did look over at Britney laying on her back.

Britney slowly lifted her head and shoulders, propping them up on her elbows. The creature was watching her as its muzzle curled back, revealing sharp, bloody teeth. She knew this had to be a War

Wolf, but where did it come from? She had heard they were all dead.

The beast was illuminated intermittently by the flashing lightning. It had the head of a wolf and a disproportionately muscular, bull-like body that resembled a man's, somehow. It had black, bristly fur, which Britney wanted to pick out of her teeth, but she was too terrified to move. Then, the creature stirred and began to rise. It was horrifying to watch as it stood to its full seven-foot height.

The beast let out a terrifying roar, directed at the intruder. Britney scrambled backward. She realized she was still on the ground, but she was unable to look away from the dark creature. She felt around for her shepherd's crook. She couldn't feel it in the tall grass around her. She didn't want to take her eyes off this creature, but she had to find her shepherds crook, as it was her only protection. Then, as the lightning flashed again, she saw it, off to her left. She wrapped her fingers around the shaft and used the crook to pull herself to a standing position. She was moving slowly, because the beast looked ready to lunge toward her at any moment.

Once she was able to stand, she placed her crook in front of herself, holding it with both hands in a striking and defensive position. The beast reacted with a violent roar as it crouched into an attack stance, extending its claws. Britney saw gore dripping from the mouth and claws of the animal. Fear struck her heart; she wondered what she was doing here. This was a real threat—she wasn't sure if she could take on such a massive beast—certainly not by herself.

Sensing Britney's fear, the creature started to take bolder steps toward her. Britney looked down at the mutilated sheep at the War Wolf's clawed feet; their fur was still snow-white except for the black gore which swallowed the moonlight. She thought of how quickly this massive beast could disembowel her with those long claws, and sharp teeth. Fear overcame Britney, who shook as she sputtered a prayer to the gods.

"Please, please let the true light save me, shine through my carvings, save me gods, save me."

The Wolf let out a gargling laugh from deep in its chest.

Britney held the crook up and saw that there was no glow coming from it or her elaborate carvings. She hadn't seen them glow since she was a small child and she wondered if they really glowed back then or if it was just her imagination. When she was young, she believed she could do anything, fight anything, and overcome any foe. But now all she had was this wooden stick between her and this massive angry monster.

Fear was all that Britney felt now as everything else faded into the background. Her body and mind betrayed her, she felt sick and light-headed. Her vision started to fuzz and go gray. Then, she felt the first blow from the beast hit her right in the sternum. Britney fell to the ground, unable to take a breath. As she lay there waiting for her death, she heard the shouts of the other shepherds.

Poor Britney, but never fear: she has a lot of strength, as you will see. I'm sorry to start this story in such gory detail. Maybe it would be prudent to go back to the beginning.

THE SHEPHERD OF OLYMPUS

CHAPTER 1: THE FLOATING GRASSLANDS

"Beware that, when fighting monsters, you yourself do not become a monster... for when you gaze long into the abyss. The abyss gazes also into you."

— Friedrich W. Nietzsche

Our story begins in the floating green fields of Olympus. You heard me right, the floating green fields. You see, the grasslands of Olympus are located atop the fluffy cumulus clouds that hover above the Mountain. Many times, these floating grasslands converge and then break away again, gliding on the currents that trap them in the sky above. These unique, secret grasslands are the grazing fields for the sheep of Olympus. They are also the home of the shepherds and woolgathers who live in quaint villages embedded in these floating grasslands.

Even the lowly station of shepherd is a magical and mysterious position in Olympus. However, these are no ordinary shepherds, and they do not dwell in natural grasslands. Although it is a rare occurrence, predators have been known to seek out and devour the sheep. It is the job of the shepherds to provide safety and security to the communities, and of course, to the sheep. The shepherds of Olympus have a critical task: to protect the sheep that provide the wool that is used to weave the fabric of time and destiny.

It is also a time of change in Olympus. Faith in the gods has dwindled among the mortals, and this has impacted the power of the gods. This has trickled all the way down to even the shepherds in the floating fields. You see, traditionally the hierarchy of shepherds has everything to do with their shepherd's crook; more specifically in the carvings on that shepherd's crook and the intensity of the glowing light that comes from the carvings. Unfortunately, in recent years, the carvings have stopped glowing altogether.

There are many theories as to why this is occurring. Many believe it is because of the lack of faith the mortals have in their gods. Yet others think it is because the shepherds have lost their way and no longer hold to the old values of the Shepherd Code. No one knows for sure.

Some of the younger generations doubt that the carvings ever glowed in the first place. Most of those in power today -- this includes the individual Councils of each cloud, and the collective High Council of the Floating Grasslands, which make up the legal authority of the grasslands -- are of the opinion that the glow matters very little. They insist that the carvings themselves are the only necessary representation of who the shepherd is, what they have accomplished, and how powerful they are.

Our story focuses on Britney, who you have already met. She is a naïve true believer, and a mid-level shepherd from the village of Cellardoor, which is a midsize floating grassland. The carvings on her shepherd's crook are second to none, and have a magic all their own.

Britney's mentor, Jed, is a high-ranking official with the Council of Cellardoor. Jed took an interest in Britney when she was a new shepherd. Jed knew that Britney's carvings signified a great leader in the making. It seemed evident to everyone that knew Britney, she was destined for great things. However, this opinion would change with coming events, which Britney would not be equipped to handle on her own.

The trouble seemed to start with the arrival of Mica, the new second-in-command in Cellardoor who would bring changes no one could anticipate. This new lead shepherd came from Megladoor, one of the most significant floating grasslands. He was a bald, middle-aged, tall, sturdy-looking man with three long scars across his face. Britney was instantly impressed with him. Although the carvings on Mica's shepherd's crook were dull and unimpressive, his personality was bigger than life. He told stories like no one she had ever met. After all, Mica and his scars were a legend; he had killed the last of Ares greatest War Wolves in an intense battle which Mica barely survived, as he defended the sheep and grasslands of Megladoor.

When Mica first came to Cellardoor, he instantly saw the potential in Britney, and took her under his wing. Eventually, Mica made Britney Third, which placed her just under Mica in command over the entire floating grassland of Cellardoor.

Britney was initially all too happy to be number three in command under such a great man as Mica. Yet, as time went on, she realized something was not right with Mica. It was just little things at first. She noticed when Mica would tell the story of how he killed the Great War Wolf, the story would change depending on whom Mica was talking to. Britney tried to convince herself that this wasn't a big deal, but as the story evolved in higher degrees, she could not shake the feeling that Mica might be a liar.

Britney also suspected that Mica was using unethical means to remove opposition in the ranks.

She could never prove her suspicions. Yet, over time all of Britney's doubts seemed to be confirmed—at least to Britney. No one else seemed to notice how Mica took over as First Shepherd.

Britney watched Mica effectively destroy the reputation and credibility of the current First Shepherd, who had been a good man and longtime leader of Cellardoor. She had never seen someone systematically destroy a person's reputation. Little by little, Britney observed how comments made by Mica to key people in the council, as well as to lower-level shepherds, effectively eroded the faith people had in their once loved leader.

CHAPTER 2: LOOKING FOR HELP

Britney was conflicted about the actions of Mica and sought the advice of a high-ranking member of the council. This man held the high rank of Director of Shepherd Relations and seemed like a good man. He listened to all of Britney's concerns and suspicions. He assured her he would investigate these affairs. He also told her to have faith in the gods, and everything would be fine. But, as time went by, and things seemed to get worse, she began to regret going to the Director.

After some time, Britney followed up with the director. This time, she detected indifference from the director, and a bit of annoyance with her claims. She knew this man would be of no help. She was beginning to feel more and more frustrated with the unethical actions of Mica and the lack of interest from Shepherds Relations, so she decided to seek advice from her mentor Jed.

Unfortunately, Jed was utterly enamored with Mica and his legendary tales of defeating the great wolf on Megladoor. His advice to Britney was to support Mica and to be careful what hill she picked to die on. Jed warned her that the most important thing to her future would be to learn the unwritten rules. Jed prided himself on being politically savvy and tried to impart his wisdom on Britney. He explained, "The first rule is to never dishonor or embarrass the Council of Cellardoor. If they have faith in Mica, then you had better find a way to have faith in Mica as well."

This advice disappointed Britney. She lost faith in her mentor and stopped seeking his counsel. Britney felt she had no one to turn to. She knew that there was nothing she could do to help the long-time First Shepherd. The damage Mica had done to this man's reputation had reached the highest-ranking members of the Council. It was clear to Britney that she needed to be careful of the politics if she wanted to protect her family and her children's futures.

Eventually, everyone who once believed in the First Shepherd had lost faith in him. These same people were now spreading Mica's rumors, which ultimately destroyed the First Shepherd's reputation. Before the First Shepherd knew what was happening, he had lost his position. Mica was promoted to First Shepherd, and Britney was now the Second in command.

Although this promotion should have been a surge to Britney's confidence, it was anything but. Her faith in the Gods, the Council, and Mica continued to dwindle as she observed other inconsistencies and irregularities. Some were quite serious. For example, Britney noticed adherence to the Shepherd's Code seemed to diminish among her new counterparts in the upper levels of Cellardoor's hierarchy. She also noticed that there were no carvings in the power section of Mica's crook. Britney wondered how Mica entered top management in the first place, not to mention, becoming the First

Shepherd, without any carvings to indicate his power level or experience. This should have been impossible in the grasslands, where a shepherd's training and power level are supposed to be important.

CHAPTER 3: STRANGE THINGS GETTING STRANGER

Britney continued to observe the odd and erratic behavior of Mica, but felt powerless to do anything about it. Then, there came the day when she made a grisly discovery. She was patrolling the fields and checking in with her shepherds, when she stumbled upon a bloody patch of grass. She had never witnessed this type of scene in all her years as a shepherd. When she located Hector, the shepherd in this area, she saw that he was frantically looking in the brush and tall grass for something. She asked Hector what he was looking for. Hector informed her that two sheep had gone missing, and he could not find them.

When Britney reported this to Mica, he acted very strangely. Mica kept his cowl hooded over his head and would not make eye contact with Britney. Mica sat in a dark corner of his hut, and when she turned up the light of the lamp, Mica became angry. “NO! Turn it down," he screamed. “I have a headache.”

"I'm sorry," she said, as she turned the lamp back down. “So, what should we do about the missing sheep and the blood?” she asked.

“Hey, accidents will happen,” Mica, said. “It’s all part of the job.”

Britney frowned at this and Mica noticed the frown. Then Mica began yelling again. "None of this would have happened if you were doing your job and staying on top of these lazy shepherds."

Mica’s fluctuating attitude and personality threw Britney off balance. She did not know how to handle the situation. Before she could react, Mica stood up, slammed his fists on his table, and ordered her to put the shepherd in that region on-report. “I don’t know why I have to keep ordering you to punish these lazy shepherds,” he screamed. “Once you are finished writing the disciplinary report, you are to forward it to the Council of Cellardoor. Maybe that will get this lazy shepherd's attention."

Britney left Mica's hut with a very heavy heart; she knew she had no one to turn to for help. She also knew she must follow her orders, no matter how wicked they were. The standard and proper protocol called for an investigation, not a write-up, but Mica would not listen to reason and threw her out of his hut. He insisted that Britney had her orders, and Mica would take care of the rest. This did not sit well with her, but what could she do?

As Britney was walking back to her home, the sun was just going down and passing through the horizon of clouds. The grass was tall here, and she felt the blades lightly graze her left hand as she walked. She was troubled about having to write a report on Hector, who was a good man and a good shepherd. She wondered what this would do to Hector's reputation when the Council of Cellardoor received the report.

As she neared her village, the scene of children running and dashing in and out of the hut's recalled fond memories of her own two daughters at play when they were younger. This put a smile on her face. She looked over to her left, and saw a group of men gathering and compressing the wool. The sight of the wool stretched and compressed in the fading sunlight made it appear golden and beautiful. Her husband was a woolgatherer, and she reflected wistfully as she walked through the fields.

Being back in the village lifted her heart. The sight of children at play as their parents worked hard, struggling to provide for them, struck her heart and made her appreciate her life and what the Gods had given her. Her own two children would never have to worry about what comes next in their life. Britney's oldest daughter was already at the academy, and her youngest would be going next year. Britney had served long enough to guarantee their place in the academy, and to guarantee that they would receive their shepherds crooks. She just needed to continue to work hard and avoid trouble.

Britney remembered how proud she was when her oldest daughter, Andrea, was accepted as an initiate. How proud she made Britney when she traveled to Treelandoor to receive her tree bone crook. Britney remembered when Andrea returned from Treelandoor and showed her mother her initial carvings. Britney had been so proud to see her daughters' carvings were just as good as hers, if not better.

It is the custom of the shepherds that each initiate, on his or her 18th name day, makes the journey to Treelandoor where they are given their sacred carving knife along with a clean, unadorned shepherd's crook made of tree bone. After the journey, half of the initiates are sent directly to the fields to train, the other half are sent off to the Academy of the High Council of the Floating Grasslands to be educated and learn the sacred arts of shepherding and carving. Later, at the changing of each season, the initiates in the fields rotate with the initiates in the academy. This rotation will continue to take place each season until the initiates have completed their training and meet the standards to the satisfaction of both the First Shepherd of their home grassland and the collective High Council of the Academy.

Britney felt the pressure of keeping Mica happy to ensure her position and in turn, the opportunities of her children. Mica had total power over her children's futures in addition to Britney's own. This thought also brought worry to Britney for Hector who also had two children that he hoped to send to the academy someday. She could not help but think of the injustice of a man like Mica having power over someone like Hector. How is it right for a man like Hector, who had struggled to perfect his beautiful carvings, to be destroyed by a man like Mica, whose carvings would barely pass as a first-year initiate?

Britney wondered again, how Mica had risen so far. Your shepherd's crook tells others who you are, what you have accomplished, and what power level you hold. All initiates are informed that the worst crime they could commit would be to allow another to carve on their crook. That would be the highest form of treason, to the High Council. Because of this fact, Britney knew that Mica had no real skills. Mica's shepherds crook signified no real accomplishments. For the first time in her life, Britney began to wonder just how vital the carvings really were. She had been raised to believe they meant everything, but apparently, that was not true in the case of Mica, the new First Shepherd of Cellardoor.

Britney reached her humble home and greeted her husband, and youngest daughter. No matter how bad her day was, seeing both always lightened her heart. Her husband, Brian, was hiding what he was cooking on the stove. She tried to peek around him, but he kept telling her she had to guess. The home lit up with giggles as Brian played his game. Then she smelled it and knew it was her favorite dish: wheat noodles, and his secret sauce. This made her smile, but Brian could tell she was upset. He coaxed her into sharing. She explained about Hector and her fears of going against Mica and what that could mean for the children. Brian agreed that it was a tight spot, but told her he knew she would find a way to do the right thing.

CHAPTER 4: DARK TIMES

Finding a way to do the right thing never came to Britney, and the pressures from Mica got worse and worse. Mica had a way of wearing Britney's resolve down. When she would take a stand, Mica would turn the heat up, adding shifts, demanding that she pull double shifts to fill in for any shepherds who called off sick. She also found that Mica did not like to be alone, and required Britney to spend her off time with him rather than at home with her family.

Britney also learned that life got a lot better when she went along with Mica's demands. When she would give in and surrender, Mica would lavish her with gifts, approve time off, and lift all the extra duties he placed on Britney. This battle went on and on for Britney. It was a continuous cycle of taking stands, being beaten down, giving in and being treated like a best friend.

One day, Britney and her daughters were invited over to Mica's house for a meal. It was on this day that Mica's selfishness and greed would be revealed to her in a way that changed Britney and her children's futures forever. Looking back on the events of this day, as she often did, she could see how she had been groomed and programmed by all the erratic behavior, abuse, and gifts. It had all been part of the manipulation, but at the time of this first event, she was unaware and unprepared.

After arriving at Mica's hut, he introduced Britney's daughters to his children and told the young ones to hang out in the back room because he and Britney had some business to take care of, then they would all have dinner together.

Mica sat Britney at his table. He said he would return with something with which he needed Britney's help. She sat at the table, wondering when the kids would be able to eat, and what he needed to work on.

This was supposed to be a social visit.

Britney looked off into the backroom. The younger children seemed to be getting along. However, she noticed that Andrea was looking at her with a concerned expression on her face. Andrea smiled at her Mother, but the concern was still there, in her eyes. Britney smiled back, and Andrea returned her attention to what the younger kids were talking about. She could tell that her daughter sensed something wrong with this visit, just as she did, but she didn't know what to do now that she was here.

Mica returned with his hands full. It was a carving kit, and his ugly Crook.

This puzzled Britney, but before she could ask, Mica said, "I need your help with carving my crook," Mica explained. "I have neglected to keep up on my carvings, and I need your help to catch up."

Britney felt relief come over her. She was happy to hear that Mica was eager to improve his ugly carvings.

Mica said, "I really admire your carvings, Britney, and I want you to give me some tips on how to improve."

Britney quickly agreed; she was passionate about carving and jumped into the lessons. She began the first lesson by explaining how she thinks back on critical times in her life or times where she had to overcome some personal struggle. She then told him about how she takes time to meditate on what she learned from those experiences. Once she has thoroughly considered what she has learned, she decides how her carvings can demonstrate these lessons. She told him that he could carve something that symbolizes what he had learned or reflects the power of the experience in some way.

Eventually, she noticed that Mica was not paying attention. This frustrated her, so she worked up the nerve to ask him, “Mica, why do you seem distracted?”

He was caught off guard by her question. He quickly regrouped and said: "I am a visual learner, and I need to see it first.”

“Oh, I see,” said Britney. "Ok, let me grab my crook and demonstrate."

Mica became upset and thundered, “NO, I need to see it on my crook.”

Now Britney was the one caught off guard; she could not believe what Mica was asking.

Mica saw the look on Britney's face and quickly changed his tune, "No, no, I just need you to get me started, I am not asking you to carve for me. You can just sand it down after you carve."

Britney was relieved, as this seemed like a reasonable compromise, "Well, this is highly irregular," she said, "but I guess I can demonstrate a couple of basic techniques to get you started, then we can sand it down again." She carved some intricate and beautiful shapes that demonstrated what she had shared with him earlier.

However, this did not go well. Mica kept claiming that he did not understand. His behavior became more and more unpredictable, as he insisted that Britney continue to show him more and more examples on his crook. She loved to carve, and it came naturally to her, so she kept agreeing to his requests. Yet, when she finally handed the crook back to Mica, insisting he try, Mica became very agitated and roared, "You might as well just put the finishing touches on it."

Britney was filled with horror when she realized that she had carved an entire section of the crook. Her horror deepened when she looked up into Andrea's eyes, who was somehow standing right next to her. Britney realized she had lost herself in the carving.

"When did you get here, baby?"

Andrea looked at her mom and then over at Mica, "I heard yelling, and we are hungry."

Britney had become so used to the abusive behavior of Mica that she did not consider how this would affect her daughter. Andrea was a first-year student, and she knew the law about carving. Britney felt shame rise in her heart.

"Andrea, honey, get your sister. We are leaving as soon as I sand these carvings off."

Andrea turned to retrieve her sister; she couldn't wait to leave this hut.

Britney reached for the sanding paper, but Mica pulled all his equipment away from her and said, "Don't worry, I will sand it off, I think I have a good idea of what to do now."

Britney reluctantly handed the crook back to

Mica and said, "I am sorry, Mica; I am just not comfortable with this."

Mica had a smirk on his face; he held the crook up and admired it. Still smirking, he looked at Britney and said "Yes, you are finished for today, I will see you tomorrow."

She left his house with her two children, who were now starving, after not being offered anything to eat or drink.

CHAPTER 5: TRAPPED

The next day Mica sent for Britney. As she walked into the First Shepherds hut, she noticed that Mica was beaming with happiness.

Mica was holding his crook up in the air as he exclaimed, "You did it, Britney, you did it."

Britney was horrified to see that the carvings on the crook were still hers, and he obviously never sanded them off, as he promised.

Mica went on to explain. "The council has been pressuring me to finish my carvings, and today they were very impressed with my latest addition." Then, his smile became a bit sly as he added, "Are you ready to work? I will make it worth your while."

Britney tried to explain that she did not mind teaching him, but she would no longer carve on his crook.

"Well, I think you will," said Mica. "You already broke the rules, Britney, the hard part is out of the way and honestly, what does it really matter?"

He then warned Britney that if Mica went down, she would go down with him and so would her children's futures. This shouldn't have surprised Britney, but she was still speechless. She did not expect Mica to come right out and say it the way he did, but it was effective. She felt all the fight go out of her as she sat down at the table and began to carve.

Eventually, Britney lost all the passion and love she had for carving, but that would not stop Mica from alternately using abuse, threats, and kindness to keep her motivated.

Britney was not the only one affected by Mica's ethics and contempt for the Shepherd's Code. Many shepherds lost their jobs because they stood up to Mica, stood for the code, or offended Mica in some way. The hard part for her was that she was the enforcer of Mica's wishes. She had been raised with the Shepherd's Code, which had always informed her decisions, given her peace, and made her confident in how she led. But, working for Mica went against many of the fundamental beliefs of the code.

Britney was conflicted when she had to write up or terminate the shepherds who she felt were only guilty of offending Mica in some way. According to the Code, the person who passes the sentence must carry out the sentence. This was good, because it ensured the person really meant it. They would have to look into the eyes of the one they were accusing or punishing. Nevertheless, Mica hid in his hut and let any slight or perceived offense ignite his anger and frustration. Then, he made Britney enforce his decisions.

Britney didn't believe in the punishments, because she knew they were motivated by Mica's ambition and strange insecurities. She struggled with this day and night, and it showed in her countenance. Mica became frustrated with Britney's moping around and looking miserable all the time, so he took her aside.

"Britney, I can't stand to see you take it so hard,

it makes me uncomfortable."

Mica went on to give her some advice. "You know Britney, you have the potential to be a great leader someday," Mica said. "But you have to get over your feelings and naive adherence to this code."

"The code is what actually keeps my feelings in check and helps me make rational decisions," she returned.

Mica shook his head, "No, they are holding you back. It's not your fault," Mica continued, "You have always been here on Cellardoor, you were raised in a small, unsophisticated village and you are inexperienced to the way things really work."

Britney listened to Mica with interest; some of what he was saying made sense to her.

Mica seemed like he was really interested in mentoring her as he went on. "You know Britney, I am really helping you out by giving you the dirty work and distasteful tasks."

"Helping me?" she asked.

"Yes, helping, you see, the more you punish, the more the shepherds will fear you. It is their fear you need, not the love they have for you. Without fear, you will never really be able to lead these men and women. They are entirely too familiar with you, and I am trying to break that up, so you need to trust that I have a plan, and I have your best interests in mind."

"What about the Code?" Britney Asked.

"You and your code. Don't you know there is more to this work and life than the code?" Mica stood; he was getting angry again. "You really are a small cloud simpleton aren't you," he turned his back on Britney. "Sometimes, I think I am wasting my time investing so much in you. I had hopes that you could officially be named the number two of Cellardoor."

"What do you mean?" she asked. "I am the number two of Cellardoor."

"Well, yes, you are filling in for that position, but it is not official yet."

Britney then knew that her position was in jeopardy. Mica's insinuation was loud and clear to Britney, she needed to get on board, or she would be replaced like so many others. Brittany reflected on the advice of her mentor Jed. She was starting to second-guess herself and the Code. She knew she was on her own with no support. She decided to listen to what Mica had to say.

"Don't worry Britney it will all work out; you just need to follow orders," Mica said. He could see that he had broken through to Britney. "Don't worry it will all get easier the more you do it" He was not only referring to the unsanctioned carving, but also to the write-ups, and dismissals that devastated the lives of the people she had grown up with, and known all her life. She could not see what she could do to stop Mica.

It seemed that the conventional wisdom of Cellardoor was shifting, and Brittany needed to figure out how to get on board with this shift. Britney found that Mica's advice was accurate. It did become a little bit easier as she stopped resisting the orders given by Mica. Though they went against the Shepherd's Code and her personal code, it all became more manageable. Although, something inside of her became restless and frustrated. Something inside her did not accept what she was doing, and this conflict within waged war on her soul.

The once happy and joyful cloud of Cellardoor

became a dark and dreary place. Many shepherds left to work at other grasslands. Those who stayed would not pick up additional shifts. The fear was, the more they worked, the more opportunities they had to be put on report. Morale was down, sick calls were up, and Britney caught trouble from both ends.

Britney found it challenging to keep the shepherds motivated with the erratic and crazy behavior of Mica, the First Shepherd. He would behave as a vengeful, angry leader one minute, and the next minute he was trying to get chummy with the shepherds. Sometimes he would cry, and tell stories about how hard life had been for him. He was adept at manipulating people with emotion. She found she would fall for Mica's tricks, even when she knew they were falsehoods.

Britney knew she could not take a stand against the First Shepherd without risking everything she had worked for. She wished there was a way to expose Mica, but nothing seemed possible. She watched Mica take down every person who stood up to him. She also knew that Mica was far better at convincing people to believe him than she ever was.

Britney thought that the council would surely step in, with all the devastation in the land, but Mica spun everything to his advantage. He explained away all the discipline and morale issues. He said this was all necessary to clean up Cellardoor and root out the lazy shepherds. Mica also used the fact that mysterious predators were attacking the sheep as an excuse to enforce tighter discipline. The council seemed to believe that all the drastic measures Mica took were because of the heightened security needs of Cellardoor.

CHAPTER 6: IMMORTAL BREAKDOWN

Britney felt hopeless and lost. She did not know how to accept and deal with all these pressures. As the pressure built, she began to experience symptoms not common to immortal shepherds. Illness was not usual in the grasslands, but when it did occur, the people went to the healer, a man who most referred to as the Herb-man.

Britney explained as much as she could to the Herb-man without compromising Mica or herself. The Herb-man told her that she needed a long rest. He took her off work for a month, and told her to stay with him in the east fields recovery center while she recuperated. The Herb-man was a kind and gentle man who knew a lot about the physiology of the shepherds. He warned Britney that she was burning through her life force too fast. He helped her see that she had to take time for herself and her family or the life force would not replenish itself.

Britney found it very difficult to slow down. She had been keeping an incredible pace for so long. As she was forced to rest in the vast east fields, she noticed that she loved the simplicity of this area. She began to take stock of the smaller things, the colors, the insects, the rocks and grass. It had complexity and beauty all its own. She also discovered that she loved to go for long walks in the east fields, .The sky was so abundant here, and the night was filled with stars, and a vastness that swallowed Britney and her troubles.

One night, as she was on a walk, she met an older man who seemed vaguely familiar to her. They both greeted each other and sat in the grass to rest. Britney took out her sacred knife and began to whittle on a piece of wood she found. The older gentleman commented on her skill. Then he said something that stunned Britney.

"Don't forget to keep your work site clean. If you let the shavings pile up, you will misread the grain."

Britney had heard this before. She looked at the old man, trying to puzzle out how she knew him.

"Where do I know you from? Have we met before?" she asked.

"Yes, we have met before. I am surprised you remember; you were so small."

Then it came to Britney. "I do remember you. I learned to carve at your feet when I was tiny."

"Yes, you did, and you have certainly improved since then," the man replied.

They both chuckled and spent time catching up under the clear, starry sky. Britney remembered that the old man was a shepherd too. She would visit with the Old Shepherd a lot when she was a child. She had begged the man to teach her how to carve, because she wanted to be a shepherd when she grew up. They reminisced about many wonderful times and happy memories.

Britney felt comfortable enough with the Old Shepherd to share her current troubles and her sadness. The Old Shepherd listened, and comforted Britney. He told her that she had some more tough times ahead of her, but he knew she could overcome this setback in her life. "Don't grow tired of doing what is right," the Old Shepherd said. "You will be lifted up in honor when the time is right, as long as you don't give up."

Britney didn't think the Old Shepherd understood how impossible her situation was.

The Herb-man approached, but stopped well clear of where she and the Old Shepherd sat talking. She noticed the Herb-man, and waved him over to join them. The Herb-man instead put his hands to his mouth and yelled, so he could be heard over the breeze and rustling grasses.

"Come back to the hut when you are done. I have a remedy prepared for you, but it will not keep long."

Britney waved her agreement to the Herb-man, and told the Old Shepherd she had to go. They hugged each other in farewell. She watched as the Old Shepherd headed east into the tall grass, until he faded entirely into the darkness.

CHAPTER 7: RETURN TO DARKNESS

After Britney had spent a month with the Herbman in the east field, she was cleared to return to work. Mica was so happy that she had returned. He told her how hard it had been to fill in for her. He also confessed that he was scared the entire month that she would give him up and tell the council about all the things he had done. Mica asked her if she told anyone about the carvings. Britney assured him that she hadn't, but she had come to the decision that she could not continue carving for him. Mica was so relieved that he agreed, and said he was just happy that she was back and healthy. However, Mica could not even make it through Britney's first day back without pressuring her to carve again. She was strong, and resisted Mica.

The trouble began again in earnest as Britney continued to defy Mica's requests to carve for him. At the end of Britney's first day, she was happy to return home and see her family. Mica waited until she had walked all the way home before sending a messenger, ordering her to return to work. The pressure was on; the abuse, threats, and kindness had started all over again, but she was determined to push through and continue to do what she thought was right. The conversation she had with the Old Shepherd stayed with her, and she drew strength from it for a time.

Pressure of another kind was on Britney now. The attacks on the sheep had increased, and the Council of Cellardoor wanted solutions to this problem. This responsibility was passed down to Britney, who was already overwhelmed with morale and staffing issues. Because of all the turnover, the shepherds were now trying to watch over flocks three times their previous size.

The biggest problem was Mica and his involvement in the planning. Britney wanted to establish patrols that would fan out and cover more ground, but Mica insisted that the men focus their attention on the areas that had just been hit. Mica was a reactionary leader, and his plan left most of Cellardoor unprotected. Britney voiced this concern at a planning meeting in front of the other shepherds. She knew it was a mistake the minute the words left her mouth. Mica laughed at Britney's suggestion, and made a few comments about her ignorance and stupidity in front of the shepherds. There were spurts of nervous laughter, but this was not the reaction that Mica had hoped for. Mica became notably upset and yelled at the shepherds; "You all have your orders. You are dismissed! Britney, I want a word with you."

Britney stayed seated, as all the shepherds filed out. When the area was clear, she walked up to Mica, who was busy studying his crook.

"You wanted to see me," said Britney, preparing herself to be chewed out.

Mica stayed quiet for a time, then he looked up at Britney.

"I know you think you have the best ideas to catch these predators, but I have done this before, and I know what to do."

"You are right," she said, "You are the only person to take on a War Wolf and survive."

"That's right Britney, so please do not interrupt me again in front of the shepherds."

She agreed and apologized. "Do you think we have a War Wolf in Cellardoor?"

"No," said Mica, "It is definitely not a War Wolf. I killed the last one, remember?"

Mica turned away from her and kept talking.

"I am not sure what the predator is yet, but I need you to support my plan so I can figure it out. Your best contribution is to take care of the shepherds, and keep them in line. Leave the actual investigative work to me."

Britney was surprised at how calm and patient Mica seemed to be after she had challenged him in front of the others. She expected to be cut to ribbons, as she had been in the past, but no one ever knew how Mica would react. Then, it all became clear. Mica put his arm around Britney's shoulder.

"Walk with me," Mica said as he pulled Britney along. "I know you are sick, and recovering still."

"Well, I feel much better," she returned, looking at the hairy arm draped over her shoulder.

"Oh, that's good," he said, "but I don't want to lose you again, so I think I have a solution to our problem."

"The attacks?" she asked.

"Attacks?" Mica asked with a puzzled look on his face. Then, he caught on to what she meant, and became irritated. "No, not the attacks, the carving."

Mica stopped, and stepped in front of Britney.

"Your daughter is in the actual Academy, maybe she can start making the carvings for me, since you're not up to it anymore."

Britney was shocked that Mica would go that far. But, Mica went even further.

"Your daughter is lucky to have a position in the academy, in this economy. A lot of kids have no opportunities to look forward to."

The threat was subtle, but clear. Britney did not know how to react, so she said:

"Well Mica, I will have to check on that and get back to you."

Mica seemed happy and hopeful at this response.

Britney could not believe this. She had no idea what to do, but she knew she would not let her daughter do this. She went for a walk; she needed to think and clear her mind.

CHAPTER 8: LOOKING FOR THE OLD SHEPHERD

The Herb-man saw Britney coming up the path to his hut; he hadn't seen her since her month-long visit. She passed his hut and kept walking. The Herb-man decided to follow her. No one came this way unless they needed medical attention. He found her standing in the east field, looking around as if she had lost something. The Herb-man approached her.

"What are you looking for my friend?"

"Hi," said Britney. "I am looking for that Old Shepherd I met here when I stayed with you, have you seen him?"

"No," said the Herb-man. "I haven't seen any shepherds out here in the east field for years. There are no sheep here, the grass is too tall."

"You misunderstand me," Britney turned and walked closer to the Herb-man. "I am looking for the Old Shepherd that I was talking to the night when you came out and called me back to your cabin. Surely you saw him, we were sitting right here in this very spot."

"I saw no old shepherd."

Britney looked at the Herb-man as if he lost his mind.

The Herb-man was also looking at her the same way.

"You never saw me sitting, right here," she pointed to the ground, "talking to someone?"

"Well, yes," the Herb-man scratched his head. "I did, but it was not an old shepherd."

"Who did you see with me then? Maybe he didn't look like a shepherd to you."

The Herb-man chuckled, "The person you were talking to did not look like an old man or a shepherd, she was a young woman."

A young what? Britney asked, stunned.

With a huge smile on his face the Herb-man continued, "She was beautiful and reminded me of someone I haven't seen since I was a small boy."

Britney gawked at the Herb-man, unable to comprehend what she was hearing. She decided to illustrate the scene again, giving much more detail. She described a man in the leather pants and poncho traditionally worn by shepherds. She described his physique, the white beard, and kind eyes of the Old Shepherd. Finally, once she was satisfied that she had thoroughly defined him, Britney asked the Herb-man how he thought the Old Shepherd was a young woman.

The Herb-man looked down in thought. He scratched his head again, then he looked up at her with a twinkle in his eye.

"Well you know, I did find it strange. The woman was far too young, but she looked just like one of the healers from my village that I knew when I was a small boy." He shook his head and said, "No, you'll just think I am crazy."

Britney encouraged him to continue, her frustration replaced with curiosity.

"She used to spend time with me and even set my broken leg once, when I was trapped in a ravine.

It is a long story, but the young woman you were talking to was the spitting image of the woman I knew. I almost ran to her, but then I could see she was talking to you and I thought it just couldn't be her. The girl I knew would be much older by now. But I can tell you, Britney, that she is the reason I became a healer and an Herb-man. All I know is that was not an old man or an Old Shepherd you were talking to that night, it was most definitely a young woman."

Britney wondered why the Herb-man saw this woman and not the Old Shepherd. All she knew for sure now was that she needed to speak to the Old Shepherd. She desperately needed advice; she had no idea what to do.

Britney stayed in the east field as long as she could. The sun was sinking below Cellardoor in brilliant reds and golds. She knew she needed to head back for the patrol that night. All the shepherds would be waiting for her. She thought of how useless concentrating all their effort in one small area would be, but she had her orders. With a last desperate look around the tall grasses for the Old Shepherd, she turned and headed back.

CHAPTER 9: THE WAR WOLF

The long walk back was good for her. She decided to keep coming back to the East Field until she could find the Old Shepherd. Britney could put off answering Mica about her daughter carving his designs for a few more days. She also thought the walk back could serve another purpose. She could now, at least, patrol some of the fields neglected by Micas ridiculous strategy.

The sun was almost all the way down as she walked, and the skies were turning dark with a coming storm. Britney loved the storms. The lightning lit up the neighboring clouds completely, turning night into day for a few seconds at a time.

It was full dark, except for the lightning to the sides, and the full moon above, before Britney reached the first grazing field. She heard some grunting noises, and then a terrified bleating. It was the sound of sheep under attack. She was running so fast toward the sound of the attack on her sheep that she ran headlong into something she had never seen in the grasslands before. The monster was busy devouring its prey. She ran into it so hard that she bounced off the creature, and landed on her back, in the grass. The massive animal seemed unaffected by the sudden impact. It barely took notice of the disturbance, but did look over at her laying on her back. Britney slowly lifted her head and shoulders, propping them up on her elbows. The creature now gave her its full attention as its muzzle curled back, revealing sharp, bloody teeth. She knew this had to be a War Wolf, but where did it come from? She had heard they were all dead.

The beast was illuminated intermittently by the flashing lightning. It had the head of a wolf and a disproportionately muscular, bull-like body that resembled a man, somehow. It had black, bristly fur, which Britney wanted to pick out of her teeth, but she was too terrified to move. Then, the creature stirred and began to rise. It was horrifying to watch as it stood to its full seven-foot height.

The beast let out a terrifying roar, directed at the intruder. Britney scrambled backward. She realized she was still on the ground, but she was unable to look away from the dark creature. She felt around for her shepherd's crook. She couldn't find it in the tall grass around her. She didn't want to take her eyes off this creature, but she had to find her shepherd's crook, it was her only protection. Then, as the lightning flashed again, she saw it off to her left. She wrapped her fingers around the shaft and used the crook to pull herself to a standing position. Britney was moving slowly because the beast looked ready to lunge toward her at any moment.

Once she was able to stand, she placed her crook in front of herself, holding it with both hands in a striking and defensive position. The beast reacted with a violent roar, as it crouched into an attack stance, extending its claws. She saw gore dripping from the mouth and claws of the animal. Fear struck her heart; she wondered what she was doing here. This was a real threat—she wasn't sure if she could take on such a massive beast—certainly not by herself.

Sensing Britney's fear, the creature started to take bolder steps toward her. She looked down at the mutilated sheep at the War Wolf's clawed feet; their fur was still snow-white except for the black gore which swallowed the moonlight. She thought of how quickly this massive beast could disembowel her with those long claws and sharp teeth. Fear overcame Britney. Trembling, she sputtered a prayer to the gods.

"Please, please let the true light save me, shine through my carvings, save me, gods, save me."

The Wolf let out a gargling laugh from deep in its chest.

Britney held the crook up and saw that there was no glow coming from it, or from her elaborate carvings. She hadn't seen them glow since she was a small child and she wondered if they really glowed back then or if it had just been her imagination.

When she was young, she believed she could do anything, fight anything, and overcome any foe. But now all she had was this wooden stick between herself and this massive angry monster.

Fear was all that Britney felt now, as everything else faded into the background. Her body and mind betrayed her. She felt sick and light-headed. Her vision started to fuzz and go gray. Then, she saw a dark blur in the corner of her eye and felt the first blow from the beast. She felt an explosion of pain in her chest. Then, she was falling to the ground, unable to take a breath. She looked up into the face of the beast. Time seemed to slow—lightning lit the features of the animal——then she saw it—across the face of the creature were three dark scars. She hit the ground, hard. Britney was devastated by this revelation. As she was laying there, waiting for her death, she heard the shouts and commotion of the other shepherds coming to her aid. Before she lost consciousness, she saw Mica take off into the tall grass, running on all fours.

Britney awoke in the Herb-man's cabin. She sat up too fast, and almost lost consciousness again.

"Hold on Britney, you need to lay down a bit."

"No," she said. "I have to get to the council; I know what is killing the sheep, and Cellardoor, for that matter."

"Well, that is all good, but you need to lie down until you are better," the Herb-man said, as he gently pushed her back down on the bed. "You lost a lot of life force tonight, and it will take time to replenish it. If you don't, you may never get it back."

Britney did feel utterly weak and unable to stand.

"He didn't even wound me," she moaned, "why am I so tired and weak?"

"Well Britney there are more than physical wounds. There are wounds of all kinds and yours are extensive."

"That may be true, but I need to get to the council. Isn't there some herb you can give me?"

"Yes, many, but they will only mask the injuries. You will need to rest, and find your source again if you hope to fight whatever is in the fields."

Britney thought to herself how valid the words

of the Herb-man were, but all she had known of her source did not help her in the field against the Monster. All she had learned only made things worse. Her carvings did not glow when she needed them most. What was her source? Did it exist at all, and if so, where would she find it?

“Ok,” she said. "Give me the herbs, and I will look for my source, but I have to start fighting now."

The Herb-man gave her the remedies and the instructions. Britney took the medication and lay back down on the Herb-man’s table. She was already feeling stronger, she felt ready to take on this fight. She had no doubt who was responsible for the attacks in the once beautiful and peaceful Cellardoor. It was the same person who was responsible for so much pain and suffering in the land. She needed to go to the council and convince them. But first, she would rest a bit as she thought up a plan of action.

Britney considered how all this happened. She felt sick for her part in all of this. How could she have been so blind, so stupid? She wondered who would believe her. It sounded crazy; the First Shepherd was the beast attacking the sheep. She doubted she could find anyone willing to listen, after they had all ignored her warnings about Mica before.

Britney decided that she would have to tell her family first. She would need their support, and she would need to protect them. Her older daughter was in the Academy, and Britney wondered how this would affect her. As she lay there on the table in the Herb-man's cabin, she heard the door burst open, and she soon discovered that she did not need to worry about Andrea. Andrea had run all the way to the Herb-man's cabin to tell Britney she would rather have her mom than a shepherd's crook. She was on board for this fight. She had always known something was wrong with Mica.

Brian, her husband, was just as supportive. Britney had to take her crook out of his hand and stop him from marching over to Mica's hut and killing him right then and there. She convinced Brian that they had to do this the right way, or it would never end. She knew that Mica's supporters were not aware that he was a War Wolf. Nothing would change if they didn't expose him the right way, according to the Code. They agreed that their hearts had to stay in the right place.

CHAPTER 10: THE COUNCIL OF CELLARDOOR

Approaching the Council of Cellardoor did not go as Britney had planned. They would not see her. She was forced to communicate through correspondence. In her letters, she laid out her concerns about Mica. She explained that she and her family were now in danger because she knew what Mica was. When she did get a response, it was worded in cold legal terms. None of the responses from the Council of Cellardoor addressed her requests for protection for her, or her family. Eventually, they stopped corresponding with her altogether.

Mica had moved fast and first while Britney was recovering from the attack. She heard from fellow shepherds, who were still loyal to her, that she had become the focus of the investigation. She soon found herself in a world of hurt. They accused her of inflammatory accusations, and trying to take the position of First Shepherd for herself. Then, she was accused of being the one who had killed the sheep, since she was the only one at the scene when the shepherds arrived.

Mica had started his campaign to discredit Britney as he did when he overthrew the original First Shepherd. He told everyone that he and Britney were close friends. He convinced almost everyone that she did not know how to balance friendship and work, and was trying to take advantage of Mica's kind nature. Mica told everybody that she had become more and more rebellious, and that her accusations were just an attempt to discredit Mica. He went as far as to say, "Next, Britney will be saying that she engraved my carvings and did all the work around here."

Most people had seen her, and Mica spend so much time together that no one doubted Mica's lies. Moreover, all the dirty work Mica had been training

Britney to do had effectively turned most of the community against her. They blamed her for the misery of the land, since she was the face of all Mica's absurd orders.

Britney realized, all too late, that her complicity with all of Mica's strange and unethical orders, as well as carving on Mica's crook, compromised her credibility. She did not know how to convince these people that a very cunning and strategic War Wolf was disguised as the leader of the community.

Ultimately, Britney was dismissed from duty as the Second Shepherd and told that her daughter would be removed from the academy, and that her youngest daughter would never attend the academy or receive her crook. The disappointment of her youngest daughter Rose was her biggest hurt in all of this. Rose had been looking forward to the academy her whole life.

Britney's only recourse would be to file a formal complaint with the High Council of the Floating Grasslands. She was warned that if she were not able to prove her accusations, she and her family would be banned from all the grasslands.

Britney kept going back to the East Fields looking for the Old Shepherd, but she never found him. One night the Herb-man came out to where she stood in the East Fields looking out over the vast sea of Grass. The view was beautiful this time of day, as the sun sank into the clouds. The breeze moved the grasses, giving them the appearance of waves in a sea.

Britney noticed the Herb-man step up next to her.

“He’s probably not coming back.” said the Herb-man looking out over the tall grass with her.

Britney didn’t want to give up hope, but a small part of her agreed with the Herb-man.

“What do you want from this Old Shepherd of yours?” asked the Herb-man.

“I just need his advice, now more than ever.”

“Does he give you advice often?”

"No," said Britney. “I only saw him that one time,” she paused and added, "other than when I was a small child.”

“Oh, well, it must have been a good talk that one time to make you come back here day after day looking for him.”

"Yes, it was a good talk," she shot back.

"Well, if you don't mind me asking, what did he tell you?"

"We talked about many things," she paused. "It's hard to put into words. I just know he would be able to help; he would have the answers."

The Herb-man asked Britney, "What did he tell you last time? Did he give you any advice?"

Britney smiled and let out a small laugh. "No, not really. I was carving on a small piece of wood, and he told me to be careful of letting the shavings pile up, or I would not be able to see the grain pattern of the wood."

"Well, that is certainly good advice," said the Herb-man a little confused. "But, I don't see how that is relevant."

"Maybe not," she paused and thought for a minute. "But, maybe it is relevant. He told me something else after that. It comes from the Shepherds Code, I think. He said that times would get tough for me, but I was to never tire of doing what is right, and at the proper time I would be lifted up in honor, if I don't give up."

Britney's voice had an excitement to it now.

Then, she turned to the Herb-man with a big grin on her face.

"Herb-man! You are a genius," she said in an excited and joyful voice.

The Herb-man was really confused now, but Britney's enthusiasm was contagious, and he found himself feeling joyful too.

"He must have known somehow, and given me what I needed," she said. "Thank you for reminding me. You truly are a healer."

Britney started running for home, leaving a baffled Herb-man standing in the east field with a confused smile on his face.

Britney knew what she needed to do now: she needed to file a formal complaint with the High Council of the Floating Grasslands, so she did. She found the next season of her life to be a living hell. She also found herself wishing the Old Shepherd had warned her more about how much dishonor she would have to suffer before she would be lifted. Or, for that matter, how much pain her family would have to endure. Not that it would change her mind.

Britney had to do what was right. She had put it off for too long. She also had to take responsibility for her compliance and compromise.

The Council of Cellardoor came at Britney and her family full-force, in defense of their reputation and the First Shepherd Mica. A date for the first official hearing was set for the beginning of winter. This gave both sides time to gather evidence and interview witnesses, including each other. These interviews were extremely hard on Britney. Endless badgering and the demands of Mica's representatives devastated her, and wore thin on the family.

Mica had the backing and all the resources of the Council of Cellardoor. This afforded him the resources to hire the notorious Hades Defenders, who imposed a hellfire and brimstone scorched grasslands approach. They rarely lost, because they used intimidation and unethical techniques to wear down and destroy their opposition.

The Council of Cellardoor looked the other way as Mica employed these demonic defenders. As far as they were concerned, Britney and her family deserved this continuous torture for breaking the unwritten rules, and attempting to discredit and embarrass the Council of Cellardoor.

CHAPTER 11: BRITNEY V CELLARDOOR PRETRIAL CONFERENCE

After a time that seemed interminable, the pretrial conference was set to happen. This would be the final meeting before the hearing at the High Council. The pretrial conference was held in the large marble atrium at the Council of Cellardoor's palace. The room was massive and beautiful. The high walls and arches were made of solid marble, in earth tones of light brown and tan, with white veins running through them. A massive tree bone table was set in the center of the room with tree bone chairs placed around it. Britney walked in and took a seat. Others from the council arrived and took seats around the large table. Jed, Britney's Mentor, appeared and took a seat as well, without looking at her. Then, Mica entered the room with his Hades Defenders. The Hades Defenders were sleazy, demonic-looking creatures that slithered more than walked to their chairs.

All parties were present. This was supposed to be an opportunity to find a resolution without having to publicly go before the High Council of the Floating Grasslands. It was also a chance for the Council of Cellardoor to settle, and avoid having every gritty detail revealed to all the grasslands.

Accusations were flying, and discord erupted from the Hades Defenders. Mica was seated just across the table from Britney. He had a smirk on his face, and shook his head when he made eye contact with her. Being back in his presence had a profound effect on her. Britney felt so much dread she thought she would cease to exist right then and there.

When the council addressed Mica and asked him about the accusations Britney brought against him, Mica did not answer. Instead, he spoke of his misfortunes at Megladoor. He told stories of his mother and her death, and he cried in front of all the council. His story was moving, and even Britney started to feel sad for him. Then, he went on to explain how he came to Cellardoor and took her under his wing. He gave an example after example of things he had done for her and her children. She could not believe the lies that Mica was telling, and it snapped her out of the spell Mica had on the room.

Britney was angry and fearful; she could see how the council members were buying this story. She could see how they were ignoring the facts and the evidence that showed who Mica really was because they were suckered in by the emotion. It felt hopeless to her.

Then, a loud crack silenced the room. Britney looked to the entry of the Atrium and saw the Old Shepherd with his glowing crook. She looked to the base of the Old Shepherds crook and saw that it had shattered the marble floor where it touched. That must have been the sound that silenced the room.

The Old Shepherd walked into the room like he owned it. "Can I have my seat back?" he asked.

The Leader of the Council of Cellardoor stood up from the seat at the head of the table. He seemed very nervous as he sputtered, "My apologies, Zeus, it has been so long we thought you weren't coming anymore." He began wringing his hands and bowing. "The Chair is yours, my lord, it has always been yours."

Britney wondered why the Leader of the Council of Cellardoor was calling the Old Shepherd "Zeus."

The Old Shepherd took the chair at the head of the table.

"Gentleman," he said, with a small smile on his face. "I have not been here because I am not welcome here, so I will not stay any longer than I have to."

Murmurs of disagreement could be heard, and the leader bowed and assured the Old Shepherd that he was always welcome. He went on to explain that this marble room was built to honor Zeus.

"Built-in my honor!" the Old Shepherd stood; anger had replaced his smile. He looked up and read the two words engraved in the archway above the table, "ZEUS FIRST, Hum." Then he looked back at the Counsel Leader, "And you invite these two?" He yelled as he pointed to the Hades Defenders.

"LEAVE!" he commanded the dark creatures.

They hissed and screamed as they were forced outside the room, seemingly dragged out by invisible hands. Once outside the room, they hovered by an arch not wanting to leave but unable to step inside, either.

The Old Shepherd began walking around the table.

"This is what will be," he said in a thoughtful voice, he paused his pacing around the table and stopped behind Britney. He placed his hand on her shoulder.

"Britney has made some mistakes, which she has owned and has learned from. However, her biggest mistake was being loyal and trusting of some of you in this room and not taking action sooner, when she discovered all this."

Britney looked up into the kind eyes of the shepherd who was looking down at her. The Old Shepherd's eyes were full of concern, love, and what she thought was pride. The Old Shepherd smiled at her and continued walking around the table.

"However," Continued the Old Shepherd,

"Britney has taken action now."

The Old Shepherd stopped his pacing, and then everyone jumped in their seats as he slammed his Crook on the table.

"And none of you believed her or helped her!" He exclaimed in a grave tone. "But what I find most disturbing is that some of you at this table are too cowardly to own your part, and somehow," he said with disgust, "you are able to sit back and let Britney and her family suffer this alone."

The Old Shepherd pulled his crook free and kept walking around the table until he stood behind Mica.

"Britney has endured and overcome a great deal, I am very proud of her, so I think it is time for the real problems to be revealed."

The Old Shepherd bent down and whispered something in Micas ear, then he looked up to Britney. Still hovering at a very nervous Mica's ear, he asked Britney, "Do you have your crook with you today?"

"Yes," she said, as she reached below the table and pulled out her crook.

The Old Shepherd smiled at her as he straightened, "Nice carvings, Britney. Now, I want you to demonstrate something to this room. I want you to rest the base of your crook on the floor and hold it at arm's length."

Britney did as she was asked. She stood up and stepped back from the table, and positioned her crook as she was instructed.

"Now I want you to close your eyes, clear your mind, and think of me and what I have taught you."

All eyes were on her except for Mica who was restless and looking at his hissing and slithering friends banished to the arches.

Britney thought back to the lessons she learned at the feet of the Old Shepherd when she was a small child. She thought of the words and encouragement he shared with her back in the East Field. She considered the peace and comfort she experienced when she thought of him. Then, in bewilderment, everything became clear to her, the source, her source. She couldn't contain her excitement. Her body tingled with goosebumps as she realized who the Old Shepherd was. She wondered why she didn't see it sooner. Something bubbled up inside her, this joy and power; she lifted the crook, eyes still closed, thinking of nothing but the Old Shepherd, and she brought the crook down with all her might.

It slammed down with a loud crack that shook Britney's whole body. Or, was it the building that shook? The floor cracked beneath Britney's feet, then, she could not open her eyes as the blinding white-hot light coming from her shepherd crook washed over the room.

As the light coming from her crook settled to a glow, her eyes adjusted, and she was able to see again. The first thing she noticed was a massive War Wolf had replaced the Director of Shepherd Relations. As Britney looked around the table, she was shocked to see that her mentor Jed had also been replaced with a War Wolf. Her eyes shot over to where Mica was seated. She was not surprised to see a War Wolf slumped on the table there. The others at the table jumped up and moved away from the enormous beasts even though the creatures seemed to be dead or unconscious.

The Old Shepherd looked over to the hissing creatures outside the arches of the Atrium. With a nod of his head, the slithering creatures scurried into the chamber and grabbed the beast that was once Mica, and dragged him out of the room.

The other two War Wolves at the table were still unconscious and changing. Everyone watched in awe as the two beasts shrunk and turned back into Jed and the Director of Shepherd Relations. The Council Leader refused to look at the two changing men, preferring to believe they had always been human.

The Old Shepherd walked over to Britney. He bent down and whispered to her. "I told you, didn't I?"

"Yes, you did," she whispered back. "But you failed to mention how hard it would be to get here. Not that I am complaining; this was worth every minute."

Still bent over Britney's shoulder, the Old Shepherd sighed and said, "Well Britney, I'm sorry to say this, but this is just the beginning."

Just the beginning? Thought Britney. "But we just won, didn't we?" she asked the Old Shepherd.

"Not the way you may think, dear." He then straightened and turned to the Council Leader who was gathered with the remaining members in the corner of the room. The men were excitedly discussing a document that had just been delivered to the Council Leader. When the leader looked up, the Old Shepherd said. "You and I need to have a word."

"Yes, Zeus, as you say." The Council Leader began excitedly waving the piece of parchment that had been delivered. "Zeus, you may be interested to know that we just received the Summary Judgment from the High Council."

The Old Shepherd laughed. "You keep calling me Zeus." He turned and looked at Britney.

"She knows me as the Old Shepherd. Britney remembers me, and that is why her Crook is glowing. I might add, her Crook is the only one glowing in all the grasslands."

The Old Shepherd's eyes were blazing as he looked into the eyes of the Leader.

"You will call me the Old Shepherd."

"As you say Ze… I mean Old Shepherd, but this is important, it changes everything."

The Old Shepherd seethed, "I have no interest in what that parchment says."

"I understand Zeu… I mean Old Shepherd. My

office?" he asked.

The Old Shepherd did not respond as he started walking toward the Council Leaders office. The excited leader turned to the others present and said, "Gentlemen, please wait here. That includes you, Britney."

The Old Shepherd turned and winked at Britney before he walked out of the chamber. Britney was troubled by the behavior of the Council Leader. She looked around the room and observed all the devastation. It was not the beautiful chamber she had entered. The arches looked as if they could fall at any moment. Huge cracks could be seen in all the walls and the floor. She decided to take a seat at the table and wait. The others in the room were gathered in a huddle, no doubt discussing the events and what they meant.

After some time, the Council Leader returned alone. Britney wondered where the Old Shepherd went. Then she felt him close in a way she could not explain. It was as if the shepherd was right next to her, even though she could not see him. This was enough for her. She felt just as strong as she did when her Crook shattered the room.

The Council Leader asked the men to join him and Britney back at the table.

The leader then stood up from the table, folded his arms behind his back, and began pacing back and forth as he talked. Britney saw a gloating smirk on his face. *What does this guy have to be so happy about?* she wondered.

"Gentlemen, Mica, who brought this disease among us, has been banished from the grasslands. It is safe to say that the scourge of the War Wolves is over."

Some of the men at the table let out a cheer. The Council Leader smiled without looking up. He made a gesture with his hands to quiet the cheers and continued.

"As for you, Britney,"

The Leader stopped pacing. He looked directly at Britney. She saw a wicked gleam in the leader's eyes as he placed his hands on the edge of the table, leaned toward her and said in a cold calculated voice, "The Old Shepherd insisted that you be appointed to the council of Treelandoor where the tree bone is harvested. To oversee the trees, the honing of the crooks, and to teach the initial carvings to the visiting initiates."

Shocked gasps rang out in the room as it filled with murmurs. Britney knew this was a high honor only given to few. She could not make out what the men were whispering. She didn't know what to do or say. Now the words of the Old Shepherd made sense to her, *this is what he meant when he said I would be lifted in honor if I didn't give up, oh, thank you, Old Shepherd, this was worth all the pain and misery.*

The leader continued, with a much bigger smirk on his face. "The Old Shepherd said your children are to be reestablished in the academy with full honors. He said that you and your family are to be relocated to Treelandoor, with all the rights and privileges of a Councilman."

Britney was shocked; she heard the men shifting and murmuring again. Although the Leader's demeanor was odd as he told her these things, she became excited at hearing the news. She decided to stand and address the council. "Thank you, gentleman, I know the claims I brought to you were heavy, and I know many of you believed in Mica, but I want you to know that I hold no ill feelings toward any of you."

Many of the councilmen seemed to relax, and some even smiled at Britney.

"EXCUSE ME!" the frustrated Counsel Leader broke in. "I was not finished talking; Britney, sit down until I dismiss you."

She sank back into her chair, not sure what was happening. *Isn't this over? Surely, they see the truth now and will help my family recover from this nightmare.* But the leader's pious anger and strange behavior made bile come to the back of Britney's throat, as fear chilled her bones again.

The Leader pushed off the table and began strutting as he talked. He had been restored to his previous self-assured nature that he had demonstrated before the Old Shepherd showed up. He cleared his throat, and continued with his dialogue. "Britney, I must share with you that although your crook is glowing, this council does not accept this glow as authentic."

Some of the councilmen at the table seemed

confused as the leader continued.

"I cannot argue that the power of the Old Shepherd is great. However, he admits that he is not Zeus. Consequently, we do not acknowledge the power that illuminates your carvings as true and pure. It is tainted with your misguided belief in this Old Shepherd, which is not sanctioned by this council."

Many of the men seated at the table began nodding their heads in a self-righteous manner. Others began to verbally agree with the Council Leader, who was working himself up into a sanctimonious fit as he continued, "While the Old Shepherd has made it abundantly clear that you are under his protection. We will not honor any agreements with him or your family."

The Council Leader then stopped and addressed the members of the council. "Gentlemen," he paused and looked at each member, and then he looked at Britney and continued. "We must move forward with our efforts to protect this council."

Shouts of agreement came from the men at the table.

The Council Leader paused and dramatically

hung his head as he said, "I know we all witnessed devastating things today, but I must insist that it is also in our best interest to protect Mica as well."

Britney was astounded. How could these men who allowed Mica to deceive them, these men who allowed those vile Hades Defenders to do what they did to her and her family, still think they were in the right? How had they convinced themselves they were justified? This was a mindset she could not understand.

Britney stood up, "How can you do this?" She shouted, shaking as she stood defiantly in the broken room.

The Council Leader called the Hades defenders back into the room. The two slimy, demonic creatures slithered up behind the leader, standing imperiously on both sides of the man as he replied to her, "We can do whatever we want to do. We have received a ruling from the High Council, and you may be interested to know that according to this Summary Judgment, we are not held to the standard of mortals. As a religious organization, we are exempt from the Fair Employment Deed. Furthermore, Mica, as an agent of our organization, is also exempt."

Devastated at this twist of fate, Britney cried out, "I have been fighting for this for the last three years. I have shown you that not only is Mica a fraud, but he is also a War Wolf. I tried to get help from you many times with no avail."

The Council Leader was still smiling as he replied, "Irrelevant."

Her shoulders slumped, she sounded deflated as she asked, "But what about the fact that Mica was the one killing the sheep and destroying the lives of so many people who got in his way? How can all you have allowed to happen to me, and my family, be okay with you? It is still wrong. Regardless of your exemption, one family should not have to bear all the costs of ridding Cellardoor of Mica. You must know this is not right?"

The Council Leader responded, "Not according to the High Council. As a matter of fact, we will now be coming after you and your family once again for the costs of damages to this Chamber, and for the high price of the Hades Defenders that you forced us to hire. You chose to bring this claim, and you decided to take on this fight."

Britney bent and picked up her crook. The domineering demons shrank back at the sight of the glowing staff. She then turned and walked toward the exit of the room, feeling more devastated than at any time in this entire nightmare. How could they see the truth and still threaten her family and her? Why wouldn't they embrace the truth and let it heal them and the land? Why destroy her for bringing it out? She realized just how naive she had been to believe these men would do the right thing.

Before she reached the doorway, she turned back and asked in a small voice, "What about the Shepherds Code? You may be exempt from the Fair Employment Deed, but what exempts you from the Shepherd's Code?"

The Leader, still flanked by the hideous demonic creatures waived the parchment above his head as he crowed, "This Summary Judgment my dear. Now get out of here; we will be in touch about your debts."

She turned and walked out, defeated, as she heard the laughter in the room behind her. *Lifted up in honor—indeed,* she thought to herself sarcastically. Her faith had been crushed. She looked down at the glowing crook in her hand and wondered, *how can it glow when I don't feel any confidence right now?* She had never felt less belief, and she had never been more disappointed with the Shepherd's Code and the system set up around it.

CHAPTER 12: TREELANDOOR

When Britney got home, she explained her devastating loss to her family and what it meant to them. They would have to find a new community, a new way to make a living, and the kids would not have the opportunities she had sacrificed so much for. More, her oldest daughter would not be able to return and finish her lessons at the Academy.

She looked into the eyes of her family members; they were not filled with the sadness she expected. If anything, there was a sort of joy.

"What is wrong with you guys," she asked. "I just told you that they are going to go forward with trying to destroy us to protect themselves."

Their smiles got bigger. "I don't understand you all. We have lost everything we have worked for, and they will win because they are bigger, stronger, and have endless resources. It is so wrong."

Her oldest daughter laughed out loud this time. Her husband placed his hand on Britney's shoulder. "You have a visitor, honey. He is out back."

She got up wondering who it could be. As she stepped outside, she saw the Old Shepherd. He was sitting under a fig tree, whittling on something with his sacred knife.

"Come, sit with me, Britney," he called as he covered what he was working on.

She sat next to him and let out a long sigh. "Well, after you left, they pretty much gloated about their victory with the Summary Judgment, and the fact that they are exempt from common decency or legal accountability. We lost, even though the truth is on our side.

The Old Shepherd giggled softly.

"I'm glad you find this funny," she snapped.

"There is no such thing as truth to people like that, there is just what they want or need. Anyway, it doesn't matter. We are moving to Treelandoor," the shepherd said as he slid the object, he was working on behind his back.

"We?" she asked

"Yes, we."

"But they laughed at all your suggestions."

"Yeah, so, we go another way. I have some connections on Treelandoor still. I have arranged for you to be a teacher to the new initiates. They have heard about you on Treelandoor, and can't wait to have you teaching the young students how to carve and find their source.

"You are coming with us?" asked Britney.

"Yes, if you will have me."

"You bet we will have you."

"Great, your family seemed to really like the idea too, and I really like your family." The Old Shepherd said as he tried to shift to a more comfortable position.

"What are you hiding behind your back Old Shepherd?"

"Oh, it's a gift I have been working on."

"A gift for whom?"

"For you, Britney, do you want it?"

"Of course, I want it," she said, as she tried to

see the hidden carving.

The Old Shepherd pulled the gift out from behind his back. Britney let out a gasp as she saw the carving. It was the most detailed carving she had ever seen. It was a likeness of her, back in the council chambers, at the moment she shattered the floor with her crook. The shepherd had even caught the powerful look on her face, and the cracking floor, with debris shattering all around her. The sculpture was spectacular. It seemed to be more than just a mere carving. It captured the true essence of her personal power. Even though she felt weak and vulnerable inside at the time the sculpture depicted, she, for the first time, could see how the Old Shepherd saw her. This revelation was enlightening and empowering in a way she couldn't understand, but a way she really liked. Britney sat there with the Old Shepherd reflecting on how much she loved having him in her life now. She let the disappointments and pain leave her heart and mind, and began to focus on her upcoming move to Treelandoor and her new life.

The move went smoothly. Britney had settled into her new job and community well. She was now able to do what she loved, and help others find the same passion she had for carving. There was still the heaviness of all she had gone through, and everything she had lost hanging over her head, at times. There was also abuse still flung her way by the Hades Defenders and Cellardoor, but she now had peace, despite all the pressures.

Every day she woke up, she was grateful that she no longer had to work at Cellardoor, or deal with the leadership there. She still felt for the people who remained there, but she knew she did the best she could for them. All in all, Britney came to find that the worst day at Treelandoor was now a true gift in comparison to the best day at Cellardoor.

Her family thrived now. Her children found other academies, and they found ways to get accepted on their own. The family would have to find a way to pay for this now, as it was not a part of the benefits package like it was back in Cellardoor. However, they all agreed that nothing was worth the cost of working at Cellardoor. Moreover, their new family member, the Old Shepherd, seemed to always have an answer or the resources they needed as challenges presented themselves.

In her new role, Britney met every fresh initiate when they traveled to Treelandoor. She never missed an opportunity to help them find their true source. She loved helping them develop the tree bone and hone their bright new shepherds crooks, as they studied under her during their Treelandoor commission.

It was not long before Britney had become one of the most popular instructors ever, in the hearts and minds of her students. She didn't even realize how much they honored her. She reflected on the time she desired nothing more than to be lifted up in honor, as the Old Shepherd had promised. However, the actual event did not take place as she had imagined. It just happened one day inside the home they had made on Treelandoor. She was sitting in the main room with the rest of her family, and the Old Shepherd. As she looked around, she witnessed joy and contentment on each family member's face. She felt it then: the honor, the lifting up, it was not what she thought it would be, but it was more than she could have ever asked for. She loved the way her family loved her. She was grateful for this new life that enabled her to actually experience and know that love.

As for Cellardoor, the cracks never stopped spreading from the Chamber where Britney struck her Crook. They kept spreading, throughout all the structures in the land, no matter how much money they demanded from Britney and her family. However, a strange phenomenon took place in the grasslands over time: The Crooks began to glow again. Eventually, it came to be that the younger generation in all the lands doubted there was ever a time when the crooks failed to glow.

The End.

ABOUT THE AUTHOR

What can I tell you that you don't already know from reading my other Book, *Gods In the Garden* (Go read it). I guess the basics. I am a lecturer, mentor and coach. I am a father of two daughters. A Grandfather of one Grandson (So far). I have a love of art, poetry, writing, and speaking. I love to help people find independence and self-awareness. My mission is to help others find empowerment through the devastating things that happen to us.

THE SHEPHERD OF OLYMPUS

Made in the USA
San Bernardino, CA
04 February 2020